RE:UNION

RE:UNION

GEORDIE MILLER

SNARE

Invisible Publishing
Halifax & Toronto

Library and Archives Canada Cataloguing in Publication

Miller, Geordie, 1982-, author
    Re:union / Geordie Miller.

Poems.
ISBN 978-1-926743-48-6 (pbk.)

    I. Title.

PS8626.I4484R49 2014   C811'.6   C2014-901117-2

Edited by Jake Kennedy

Cover illustration/Design by YO RODEO POSTER CO.

Interior design by Megan Fildes | Typeset in Laurentian and Gibson
With thanks to type designer Rod McDonald

Printed and bound in Canada

Invisible Publishing | Halifax & Toronto
www.invisiblepublishing.com

We acknowledge the support of the Canada Council for the Arts, which last year invested $157 million to bring the arts to Canadians throughout the country.

Invisible Publishing recognizes the support of the Province of Nova Scotia through the Department of Communities, Culture & Heritage. We are pleased to work in partnership with the Culture Division to develop and promote our cultural resources for all Nova Scotians.

For G.K.C.B., with love from a grateful brother and son

RE:DEDICATION

NEOLETTRISM

Dear Ayn Rand,

Thank God you're dead, in dollars you've sewn up. For all you knew, we're all you.

Stuff the all. I'm doing me, while they do them. They do jokes about Stalin, talk sincere about anarchy.

A is A, whatever will be will be. I was behind, but now I see.

Seriously, take me. I'm in a bad state; all states are bad.

Can you lift, rising tide? Boats over the skyline suppose walls were built to fall.

I have shored these lines against an expensive grave
Freedom gone postal
Freedom to say, poetry is passé
Business won't go out of business

These letters, lyrics, look
you at your word.

RE:TURN HOME

I'M FROM ST. CATHARINES

How we had to get signed out of school
How someone told my brother that *he*
put people in boxes and cut them up
How my brother cried
How we weren't allowed to read the paper
How a Missing poster was next to
the "No Backpacks Allowed" sign
on the door of the Victoria Variety
where we bought our candy
How Dylan Green grew up next to the house
How the white Camaro supplanted the villainous blue van
How Sarah opened a detective agency at recess
How no driver could get directions from a kid in our city
ever again
How the Vice-Principal of Kristen French's school lived
across the street from us
How we had high school assemblies where her parents spoke
How it happened in a basement
How they tortured her to Bowie
How I don't listen to Bowie.

DIPLOMACY

Monday my Grade Twos made posters depicting one thing
they'd change about the world. For William it was flying
cars, Lindsay a new brother, Tommy wanted Korea and
Japan to be friends. The East Sea a green heart in his poster.
Because there was only one red crayon, Lindsay refused
to share. Her *old* brother had burst a lot of blood. Tommy
said something nasty to her in Korean.

SUMMA

The bridge goes back and forth
across Cascadilla Creek
a sublime accomplice
memorial string accessories to obstructing fences
after the fact

on the patio above the terminal point
summer students put off their calculus cramming
together though

gift shops
peddle t-shirts without irony
"Ithaca is Gorges"
and license plates with I-heart-Ithaca
except the heart is a grape

your name
among those others
sons-friends-strangers-classmates

Snort of the truck climbing the hill,
then the jack brake correcting
up, up the hill
out of here.

DISCIPLES

Dear Andrew,

You leap into my living room
scatter books and cats
gleaning
where I winter
winter I wear
words arrive slowly
bundled in hesitations.

ONE DAY OF SUMMER

See the arms with skateboards, swimsuits,
Coronas and croquet sets
or entire beaches and baseball teams
packed in picnic baskets
frisbees, tanktops, watermelons
the sun only seeks
on the one day of summer

On the one day of summer
cancel your mall plans
quit your office job
stand up your Nana for tea

On the one day of summer
shirts are, indeed, optional
"I guess shirts are optional" is forbidden

On the one day of summer
horizontal is the new vertical
grass like paper—it beats rock

On the one day of summer
don't go home
unless the third base coach decides
in which case, be prudent.

FIELD NOTES

an argument about jacket fabric we overhear in a
Greenpoint bar the way the one guy says leath-uh minister
of burritos remember the 90s paid in tequila nostalgia
is irresponsible Band of Gold jumping from couch to
couch Lightning has a tumour pay phone post-op a
letter I couldn't keep your summer job in guest rooms the
whale joke Scrabble on the church steps tickling chickens
reaping the fields tailgate the stadium lot 1918 down the
street corresponding grandparents surely these thoughts
are worth having drained in noise belt them out by the
canal sock wash sink it's a show about a family the world's
always ending Pine Tree Rd at home with what wasn't
piss rock up all night pickup lines from poets you didn't
disappoint me on a hike with Sun Myung Moon titling
unpublished biographies the l'esplanade the better strobe
light Mazda 072199 steinbeck no one should live in
the desert sessional infinitude those passages in Geuss
that call poststructuralism's bluff Jollimore leg wrestling
federation champion make that mistake as long as I'm
around wanna be liked Uncle John's mailing address
from Nana the heart is half a proverb interrogating the
Real textual evidence nicely supports your summary lost
in nothing found a solitude for two the thing is if you're
so inclined kiss the sun men's room magic mustard bag
hula non-rhythmic anonymous horizons the Council for

Bettering the Reputation of Boredom sentences made of wool warm and uncomfortable outside tents inside fences comforter arrangements recipe for dreaming about Tina Fey nap from halftime of the homecoming game until the rest lunch under a lion buses every 7 minutes moths bouncing off the ceiling beat wave doesn't trust colours porta potty intruder empty office again Androgynous final draft soundtrack would wait for her in 5am downtown violence or the promise of works necessarily uncollected work to gather evasive answers karateman cast because of snake bite romantic hopeless soy milk bread bananas tofu what else I'm Juan Gonzalez re-introduce myself tomorrow morning when I apologize sea hag grey sail the talking foie gras story my friend Jerilyn is in the Rhetoric department toxic table combinations Hemingway's quote-unquote private hell lucky for Robbie poor unfortunate souls tube times thwarted Olympic aspirations 50-plus shades of grey let it breathe one potato Andy Dalton as the third son bearplanes Super Eric what's Barbasol? absent absinthe bar wharf cat vibrator sketches Gold Bond morning plastic bag angels and Pal sisyphists Fuents be the dragon the first hole in the wall My Soul chicken flautas a pathetic rooster dinnertime clupass incommunicado

CAIN THE BARBER

There used to be a barbershop
by the bus station at Bay and Dundas
called *Terminal Cuts*.

OVERLAID

Have the fun we might
impromptu Montreal
hindsight forgets its arrival

The other man in my aisle while we idle
reading *Atlas Shrugged*
to his child.

THROUGH AND THROUGH

Through other people, our lives led
Lenin to the mountains with the *Logic*
sideways humans underground off somewhere
Ice baby's girlfriend
the American dreaming of overtime
two combinations from *Love Actually*
children with that joy joy joy down in their hearts
seen out the window of the house where we live
as shut-ins
–a man in a shopping cart pulled by pit bulls.

ANACHRONISMS

The Canada Malting silos cannot see
the woman assault her suitcase
she is in the frame
"Just fill in the empty spaces,"
a photographer friend advises

Ok.

RE:DIRECT LOVE

A RIVAL

Dear anonymous couple at Logan,

Your Customs and Border Protection line is my Customs and Border Protection line. Wrapped up in each other, you probably don't notice.

Another difference between us: your excitement about awaiting Bostons is my envy. The way the Museum of Fine Arts and afternoon Red Sox game already reside with you.

My broken engagement will be your doing. I'll tell the immigration officer that the purpose of my visit is to start a new life.

One postcard at a time.

MODERN LOVE

I'm a hopeless romantic; I like my romance hopeless. Never the bridesmaid, always the bride. My sister's boyfriends. Hegel. Whitney Houston. Plenty of fish, belly-up in the sea. short-distance runners. long-distant students. Open caskets. missing cats. Even Norman Mailer: I'm reading *Executioner's Song* on repeat—it's a love quarrel between Gary Gilmore and the State of Utah... People who don't dance.

BAGGAGE

Dear Lucy,

Ottawa flat and dull far below, as it would be around me.
Our plane's shadow a scarecrow lying prone on tree tops.
If the green fields are your face, darling, perhaps you need
to wash it.

I need to watch it. Want to deplane prematurely and
never see you again. Or choke myself with this letter I'm
writing. Drink to near-death with complimentary booze,
then pass out in a farming community outside the capital.
Stitch something pithy into my Levis and let a tractor till
me. "This body only made sense when you were near" or
"Now you can have my heart for real." Though you'll have
to ask the coroner. He's from a place where romance is
suspicious.

I suspect I am the suicide bomber
whose ends complete a sentence.
Come collect the tiny parts I've become. Assemble me again.

CEREMONY

Dearly beloved
We are gathered here today
We are gathered here today
We are gathered here today
We are gathered here today
We are gathered here today
Today we are gathered here
Here we gathered are today
Are we today here gathered?
We are here today gathered
Gathered today here we are
To celebrate
To fulminate
To legislate
To masticate
To fellate
Here
Here
The union
The looming
The rooming
The moonin'
The boon
of
this
today

gathered
we
are
beloved dearly.

DISCRETION IS THE BEST PART

Dear Vera,

The rain or otherwise
I would've walked you the rest of the way downtown,
where you said you lived
Leaving me on a curb by the Commons
imagining living room for blocks
Your bed on the crosswalk
All your kitchens menu-stocked
For nightcaps, a well shot

My mind's not so special
Having recycled the college prank
where the freshman roommate returns from Thanksgiving
to find his furniture on the quad
What the heck? Nature never wanted to be our mother, son
Pregnant with death drives and redundant rebirth
Instead the apologetic pranksters will say
Relax. We'll help you move back in, bud

Back to you
showering on the schedule of clouds
annoyed at intruding traffic
You live downtown
And—of course—you're not alone

I merely substituted the abstract for the concrete
If anyone asks
It's how I might define intimacy

Like when you talked about V.I. Lenin
by the dance floor at Cheers
I thought that you knew him
someone you went to junior high with
or a Facebook friend
What is to be done?
Surely this spirit
exhausts itself.

REGRETS OF A HARPOON-SHY HARPOONER

Just one:
I didn't catch your eye at breakfast
It landed in a falafel at not-my table
You threw your eye? A bit desperate
even for the sake of metaphor.
Then again
You pre-empted me.

MONOGOMANIA

She said I wouldn't be her last and
like, I get it
Our love exceeds what bodies need

In my head, however, in my head
Just fuck me from atop the bathroom sink
to the boy next door
with the doo wop, doo wop
that thing, that thing, that thing.

SINGULARITY

True art has *nothing whatsoever* to do with disgusting
emotional exhibitionism.
 — Slavoj Žižek, *The Neighbor*

Dear Laura,

Once upon a time
I wrote a poem after our only brunch date at *Jane's*
necessarily failing to describe your eyes
in ridiculous rapture, on my bed—scribbling

Now I'm in a bus station in Buffalo,
recalling things that I never sent

A dilemma that didn't become one

Walking the four miles from Toronto Island
to our neighborhood for the night
Following Pavement, mustard, beaches, wine boxes,
  David Foster Wallace, poutine stops. Oh, and that private ferry
"The Heat of the Moment" played
You kept quoting my line:
"Passive is the only aggressive I've got."

FOUND A REASON

Dear Joanna,

I wonder what you're doing with your body tonight. Mine's on
a couch into a novel about a guy whose in love, but can't get it
up. Paris is no remedy.

Maybe you're on the mudflats with Mr. More Right.
On everyone's knees back bench Psalm 93.
On a crosswalk supplicating bumpers.

Texts staccato in to absolve the mystery.
Dreams defer
your infidelities.
I also rise. On a train to Spain.

FIRST STEPS

Just A Jealous Guy Anonymous meets every week and goes over
what could be got over. Every thought that sentenced a spouse
and a coworker to a motel lunch break.
Every glance that dispossessed.
Every song that evoked this or that ex-lover.

There is always coffee to accompany the assurances that Cabo
can't be done in an afternoon. That we can deduce less than
nothing from Facebook.
That control ends where I begin.
That control ends where I begin.

GOING PUBLIC

Dear Shorty,

I supposes a lot. Like anyone could care how you shrouded me in holy fuck, as if Jesus was just a word for gratitude embodied, and not the guy who did good things so we don't always have to. Have to confess I don't think I'll be back, but whenever dying does it can't undo you running out to bring me in on our first afternoon. Onto the same street wet three weeks later you'll yell *I am Sheba. I know* there is no better place beyond these memories and anticipations. You know Sheba she sipped from Solomon's jar half full of what would happen. No need to plead *let's spend the night together*. More than ever I wonder whether 700 wives will be the ways we describe our life to other people. Just enough too much. Barely regal yet wise with you and I.

RE:CAST FAMILY

REUNION

Truth or Dare in woods far from the cottage. Children rarely choose truth. I dared you to pick the dandelion leaning over the cliff's edge. You went further, skidding down into branches, bloody chin. Claimed that it had been a Cops and Robbers accident.

Brothers are no authority on the lives of teenage girls. Only later did you tell me. The guy who was friends with the guys from Alexisonfire. Thought that I could shield you, like I was still on the top bunk of the bed we shared in the basement. The feet on the floor above our heads were the sound of the ceiling collapsing. Every night I saved you. And the furnace rumbling in the next room. Like a predator.

"This Machine Kills Fascists." You biked from action to action during the G20 with a cardboard sign on your basket. One of the fascists hit on you, as if anti-capitalism was a singles bar. That pig dies in our revolution, rest assured. The dream where we kill Stephen Harper and reduce Fort McMurray to rubble. Together.

ACTINOMYCES

Dear Emmett,

The first line is the hardest. Let's get past it.
It's today. The rain is gone. I've counted seven worms so far.
Two crawl into each other. I drop my apple core on someone's
lawn. I want communion. I want a word for the smell after the
rain. It gets in me; I like it. The little white dog on the too-long
leash is alive. Same as the lady in the bad sunglasses driving
the black SUV. She makes a left at the yellow light. She's alive.
The trees. Sure. When I notice that everything is alive, I notice
myself noticing this.

Spring forward. Last night, catching up. *How are you? Oh, you
know*. You said the sad thing straight. My heels stubbed the
floor. *Sorry to hear that*, hear it still. The human comedy is not
very funny. Say, what would you say? I listened. Fell behind.

Our lines hardly last. Tomorrow and leftovers and hope
beyond containing.

AIN'T HEAVY

Some San Diego pier they're walking ahead—as if it's endless.
And if it's endless they'll keep comparing blue whales with
whale sharks as if it's the only conversation people should ever
have. And, if they step off, the ocean won't end them this time.

TRAVELOGUE

The elderly couple in the seats next to me marvel at all those great lakes of Ontario below. A flight attendant interrupts—a round of tomato juice. When she jokes about adding vodka, the wife refuses. "He takes pills for his cancer."

Hours later, the plane lands and the attendant declares, "How can you not enjoy Vancouver today—green grass, sun in the sky?"

GOING AWAY

Dear Burgo,

Your reunion dues surprise me, friend. Went to the west coast
to find your family in an Olive Garden. Your cousins mistrust
menus, brought pasta in plastic bags. Can that be right?

What seems may come. We added a block so you could sketch
a stepdad, out of tunes about suburban New Jersey and World
War Two. "Independence Day," in other words. Let future
histories live up to their name. For now you play piano like
Anne Frank in the song that was on when we got back.

THE ELEMENTS OF STYLE

Use the active voice

Roland Barthes was struck by a laundry truck. Death he did do.

A laundry truck struck Roland Barthes. He died.

Express coordinate ideas in similar form

The Buffalo Bills kept breaking Dad's heart. That one where Whitney sang the anthem. Oh say we all saw the kick sail wide right.

The Buffalo Bills keep breaking Dad's heart. That one where Whitney sang the anthem and Norwood's kick sailed wide right.

Revise and Rewrite

"Hey Jud"

"Hey Jude"

Do not break sentences in two

He was an interesting talker. A man who never repeated himself.

He was an interesting talker, a man who never repeated himself.

Do not inject opinion

She's in love in Detroit.

She's in Detroit.

Do not overwrite

9 THINGS THAT YOU NEVER

Dear Grandad,

Dying was something you had never tried before
You also never:

Managed a fantasy baseball team
Days are numbered
in arbitration over mascot salaries
the dog in a trench coat
with unreasonable demands

Dropped acid
Subcutaneous rainbows
leaking in
the money's always greener

Had a surprise party
Even the unexpected
obeys narrative convention
UFOs are identified as UFOs
tame dreams humble the lottery winner

Stepped out
What becomes of wedding gifts?
the 4-slice toaster, now excessive

a felled coat rack

Played the banjo
The tickets said nothing about a hootananny
eventually current,
warnings will be
the only way

Dug canals
The day is before and after shots of light
between
hands falling, hands rising

Pulled an All-Nighter
Don't knock
Try it
Until
sky rockets return
evening   disheveled
  out   done
        already.

Annotated bibliographies
So-and-so argues
this or that

so is so
and this
not that

Peeled an avocado
Knew you were new
just the way
you gripped the chips
like they weren't alive.

MAIDEN NAMES

Dear Mom,

Your cigarette sisters, broken hearts. Already teenaged against
your becoming. Their banter in given names, like smoke
expanding. Like Troy. Like Gordy. You're under a blanket
in the next room. Reading poetry. Fire hazard flashlight. A
different dance, with Leonard.

The Leonard Hotel, before dark. Stranger exits window,
entering your life at the moment his ends. His trench coat as if
blood rains for containing. You never looked up. Night comes
to confirm you, sincerely.

Letters are not golf course patios, a lost art. One thumb stuck
out of the envelope, you couldn't fit. Hitched from Thorold to
Banff and Bobby. Hitched from then on. A story for your 25th.

My first birthday party, fits and starts. The guest list a
grave plot. Surnames a given. It almost didn't happen. The
aneurysm you thought you woke with, the middle of the night
before. How Ibsen would've plotted.

Your community theatre, sums and parts. Am I to believe the
woman on stage talking lewd is also you? Laughing like you
will later, when we discover the world absurd. Enveloped and
open, the only way.

RE:CALL CULTURE

NO HANDS CLAPPING

The little woman wanted noise. Noise did not want the little woman. It took time to prove. Her alarm clock must be broken. *I'll take it to the place where things get fixed*, she thought. Eggs for breakfast, a silent pan. The man in the shop, his lips together and apart. Her voice too was broken. All sound dropped. Animals and machines, broken broken. The world already too big with noise.

SUMMER OF '70

It was the summer of self-love
Me and some guys from school
We tried real hard
to stay inside jokes
like the one about your mama's porch
I shoulda known
we'd never get far

But when you're young, you're reckless
we made a virtue
of nothing to do
I'd lie in bed
eyes closed, oh yeah
played it till my fingers bled

It was the summer of self-love
no one got married
for the Works, we'd wait forever
holding the dough's damp hand
there wasn't no use in complainin'
you got a job to do

Man we were killin' time
aided and abetted at the drive-in,
the five-and-dime

Look at everything's that come and gone
still the sound of the six-strings
desire for ourselves and never no one else
(as if we had the choice)

It was the summer of self-love
We needed to unwind
When I look back now
there is nothing behind me
I guess nothing can last forever
I wonder what went wrong
Those were the best days of my life

OHH BABY

Dear ODB,

You were right about the raw
it wears through me
I like it too.

CONTRACTION

Dear Occupant III,

It's still and too early in the century for a landscape survey

79. Which of the following most accurately describes your
    relationship with the natural world?

A. Physical
B. Platonic
C. You first
D. Fleeting

97. One tide says to the other tide:

A. "I would go out tonight"
B. "If someone asks, this is where I'll be"
C. "The change will do you good"
D. "I've lost control again"

Poster punks in the deciduous district
TREES FOR THE FOREST
STONES BREAKS BONES
IF HE FALLS, IT'S HERE
No one is around. Two birds sling their shadows over a road.
The shoulder won't shrug.

A beautiful day there's not a cloud in the sky.
A beautiful day there's not a cloud.
A beautiful day there's not.

You should hear what the weather says about us
thunder classified comic gossip obits sun strip
all the print that's fit to noose

Campaigns to defeat and to lose
Recycle-Reduce-Rechoose
Organic Ice Cubes
Compost-Mortem
slogans packed
just in case...

Speech gets stumped
with names bygone
to indubious extinction
three candidates drone
"bees, caribou, tap-water, the great outdoors, house pets,
 penicillin"
"deerberry, seasons, wolverine, umbrellas, books"
"oak, parks, sand, constellations"

Elect the preterite.

IF YOU WANT TO

Dear Karen,

The dead don't need the writing on our walls

Lou Reed gone before the fried egg sandwiches came

wasn't aware he went on past *Berlin*

where there's a zoo, there's a real big zoo

when we go every animal will know

we're speculating upon their birthdays.

READING AS ALGORITHM

Dear twenty-first century readers,

You like Cormac McCarthy's *The Road*
I like Cormac McCarthy's *The Road*
Like the onset of some cold glaucoma dimming away the
world
Like pilgrims in a fable swallowed up and lost among the
inward parts of some granitic beast
Like a charcoal drawing sketched across the waste
Like an apparition
Like some old world thespian
Like the great pendulum in its rotunda scribing through the
long day movements of the universe of which you may say it
knows nothing and yet know it must
Like the last host of christendom
Like something fetched from a tomb, so dried and drawn
Like the dying world the newly blind inhabit, all of it slowly
fading from memory
Like a dogmusher
Like farm animals
Like certain ancient frescoes entombed for centuries suddenly
exposed to the day
Like the ruins of a vast funhouse against the distant murk
Like latterday bogfolk
Like pilgrims of some common order

Like an underground train
Like ruined aviators
Like migrants in a feverland
Like the shapes of bears
Like the northern lights
Like a grieving mother with a lamp
Like failed sectarian suicides
Like a path of basalt winding through the woods
Like a flash of knives in a cave
Like the shape of a flower, a molten rose
Like the pitch of some last venture at the end of the world
Like mist
Like stands of heathen candles
Like gaming cards
Like a fallen plate
Like a penitent
Like a ship
Like an animal inside a skull looking out the eyeholes
Like a dog
Like lepers
Like some ancient anointing
Like sappers
Like ancient documents
Like something trying to preserve heat
Like dental molds
Like a blueprint for assembly
Like wind-up toys
Like an after-image in the disturbed air

Like some hibernating animal
Like an offering
Like drunks
Like something out of a deathcamp
Like the track of some enterprise upon a graph
Like mendicant friars sent forth to find their keep
Like a dawn before battle
Like ground-foxes in their cover
Like smoke
Like a grave yawning at judgment day in some old apocalyptic
painting
Like a pile of rags fallen off a cart
Like someone trying to feed a vulture broken in the road
Like a child
Like a starved and threadbare Buddha
Like some storybook peddler from an antique time
Like shoppers in the commissaries of hell
Like squid ink uncoiling along a sea floor
Like fugitives
Like the bowels of some great beast exposed to the day
Like victims of some ghastly envacuuming
Like a cat licking its reflection in a glass
Like traffic victims
Like a house in some uncertain dream
Like skeptical housebuyers
Like a troll come in from the night
Like another dining implement
Like a thing being called out of long hibernation

Like a man waking in a grave
Like those disinterred dead from his childhood that had been
relocated to accommodate a highway
Like apes fishing with sticks in an anthill
Like the desolation of some alien sea breaking on the shores of
a world unheard of
Like a slowly heaving vat of slag
Like trains
Like an isocline of death
Like exhausting the least likely places first when looking for
something lost
Like parade horses
Like a man checking for ripeness at a fruitstand
Like icing on a cake
Like rats on a wheel
Like a tabernacle
Like formations in a cave
Like knitting
Like an orphan waiting for a bus
Like weeds in the floor of a stream.

THE RESEARCH QUESTION

It can't be the case that it's the case that can't be
Can it make sense to make sense?
It can to
if and only if
always already
ready only if
all if always and

Following from contradictions
According to distinctions
Attention paid revisions

but but but.

INAUGURAL

Bringing a black eye to my first protest
in the food court of the Mic Mac mall
to call a genocide a genocide

Lola saw her first snow this afternoon
her head upturned as if grateful
could she know where anything comes from.

POEM

Dear Frank O'Hara,

I'm trying you out in the deli. Cornered beef on rye. Might make up my mind. Your consumptive enthusiasm has me unsure. My friend Bart says it's about poetics in which case you're pathetic. The art of buying isn't hard to master. Too happy today though to turn myself into a municipal election. Spoiled ballots and too much coffee.

Then I'll decide to detour through the Public Gardens but it will be Central Park. People with their redundant get-lost sunglasses. I am! My phone buzzes with a baseball game tonight. If I ever find my way back, beyond the Frisbees, the supine yard sale. Smiling, sapped of anxiety.

SAPPYFEST

The one about the girl who snored like a mosquito. You woke up tent dawn bone sore, draped your thumb and forefinger seeking borrowed blood. She woke up in a napkin.

The ginger who ordered a double Americano at 11pm, his eyes beds unmade.

The clouds above Murray Beach speech bubbles outlining black metal murders.

The risk assumed by Las Vegas logos, emblazoned on consecutive shirts.

The way we don't talk about the ways we won't talk about.

The host's toothbrush to which bad breath entitles the guests.

The legs a row of party bros bouncing. Their rollicking rock parts. "Yeah man." Draw a dick on the mirror in the men's room, fellas.

Find yourself reflected here.

ZERO DARK THIRTY

Liberals For Torture
mean to end
counterfactuals

the bottom line
lifts all boasts
post festum haste

fundraisers suit entire
lives that quiet
constitutions

the press release
murders and worse
entertainment.

INCONSEQUENTIAL

Even my fantasies disappoint me

I acquire a second language
in exchange for my first

Rupert Murdoch dies
peacefully

A rival's dog-and-pony show
features heroic dogs and flying f-ing ponies

the writing won't stop
and doesn't improve.

FITTING IN WITHOUT BELONGING;
OR, ŽIŽEK'S ARGUMENT ABOUT
HOW IDEOLOGY FUNCTIONS

Toilet paper shortages announced in Ljubljana
do more than self-fulfill
their rumoured disappearance
panics even those who know better
the run-out's artificial
but "those stupid guys" will run out regardless
and those who don't
wipe themselves with rags for weeks.

VULGARITY

Everyone's got boring stories
the one about the first time you had a rice cake
the rationale behind discarded pet names
a recurring dream about misplaced commas

There's also mysteries no one cares to investigate:
the decision to write "just kidding"
the most expedient way to halt a ceiling fan
breaks in a food court's traffic patterns

The car ahead signals properly
a drink doesn't spill
someone takes the stairs

Someone takes the elevator
there will be weather tomorrow.

AIRPORT REFRAIN

All the gorgeous people going to Aspen are not gorgeous
I whisper this to her
She remains unimpressed by Denver
This city is an airport
and the city won't let us leave

I remind her that the Pacific Time Zone is almost always in a
giving mood
but loss outlasts gain
again and again

We respect cause and effect

Our connecting flight is just another flight, in our absence
like how a house cat drops the distinction on the street

The boy from Indiana is my stereotype of him
Midwestern behind us in a customer service line that keeps
taking prisoners
All around us, small talk grows into speculation
about pilots' stock portfolios
stuffed with airport hotels

We respect cause and effect
"Paging: Pre-boarding announcements

Pre-boarding announcements: This is your final boarding call"

We're side-by-side in the aviation theater
I watch success stories broadcast through giant windows
People take off to where they're going
to the indoors, unfortified.

HAPAX

A poem about neoliberalism
A poem about where you grew up
A poem about the year you taught English in Korea
A poem about suicide
A poem for a fellow poet
A poem about the weather
A poem that remembers
A poem as a knock-knock joke
A poem idling
A poem about your ex
A poem in transit
A grateful poem
A poem written in an examination hall
A poem impersonating Cohen
A poem for little girls who dream of being golf caddies
A poem about the cruellest month
A brunch poem
An insecure poem
Another brunch poem
A poem about a high modernist
A poem that objectifies
An entitled poem
A titular poem
A poem about grief
A poem for your brother

A poem about pleasantries
A poem about a party
A poem about politics and the English language
A poem for your namesake
A poem for your biggest fan
A poem from a children's book
A CanCon poem
A poem about knee socks
A poem about your love of baths
A poem about society of the spectacle
A poem composed of all the similes from an American novel
A poem about agreeing to disagree
A poem about Idle No More
A personal poem
A poem about a long weekend
A poem about propaganda
A poem that isn't about sabermetrics
A poem about the long century
A poem with a new title
A poem about firsts
A poem that won't last.

ACKNOWLEDGEMENTS

To Robbie MacGregor for getting the book out into the world—prudently, and with a generosity highlighted by hamburgers, educational emails, and one more cup of coffee.

To Jake Kennedy, who heard when the words wanted to become something better and helped make them sound that way, not to mention when they didn't fit and why.

To Megan Fildes, along with Paul Hammond and Seth Smith of YORODEO, for keeping Invisible's streak of making beautiful art objects alive.

To Andrew Patterson, Jenner Brooke-Berger, Kat Shubaly, Veronica Simmonds, and Corey Mombourquette, who gave me a lot of opportunities to read out loud to other humans.

And to Jeska and Herman Grue for providing a place to write and many reasons to do so.

SNARE

THE SNARE IMPRINT is home to exceptional, experimental poetry and prose. It represents part of Invisible Publishing's ongoing committment to a culture and tradition of literary innovation in Canada.

If you'd like to know more, please get in touch. **info@invisiblepublishing.com**

Invisible Publishing
Halifax & Toronto